BRITAIN IN OLD PHOTOGRAPHS

STEPNEY, BETHNAL GREEN AND POPLAR

Craft School, No. 37 Stepney Green, *c.* 1911. This house, which was featured on Gascoyne's map of 1703, is in Hayfield Passage, a narrow cobbled turning just off Mile End Road. Stepney Green is one of the old village greens surviving in East London, and both the house and its wrought iron tracery have survived remarkably unscathed since the reign of Queen Anne. The building was a Jewish old people's home in the 1890s, became the Craft School in about 1911 and was later used as Community Care Offices. Now it is called Stepney Green Centre and is occupied by the Tower Hamlets Careers Service.

BRITAIN IN OLD PHOTOGRAPHS

STEPNEY, BETHNAL GREEN AND POPLAR

ROSEMARY TAYLOR AND CHRISTOPHER LLOYD

ALAN SUTTON PUBLISHING LIMITED

Alan Sutton Publishing Limited
Phoenix Mill · Far Thrupp · Stroud
Gloucestershire · GL5 2BU

First published 1995

Reprinted 1998

Copyright © text: Rosemary Taylor and
Christopher Lloyd, 1995; © photographs:
London Borough of Tower Hamlets

British Library Cataloguing in Publication Data.
A catalogue record for this book is available from
the British Library.

ISBN 0-7509-0877-7

Typeset in 9/10 Sabon.
Typesetting and origination by
Alan Sutton Publishing Limited.
Printed in Great Britain by
MPG Books Ltd, Bodmin, Cornwall.

Cover photograph: Lincoln's Fruiterers, 644 Mile End Road, 1935, looking west, with Tillett's
Laundries next door. These shops are part of Wilby Terrace, built in 1848, adjacent to St Clement's
Hospital. The terrace is still standing and is called Gunjal House. The shop in the background, No.
640, on the corner of Lincoln Street and Mile End Road, was Max Broer, baker and confectioner.
Lincoln Street was renamed Brokesley Street in December 1937.

The Tower of London and the River Thames with the *Royal Eagle*, a Thames paddle
steamer. In the distance is the tower of the old Port of London Authority Head Office.

Contents

The consecration of the wayside cross at the corner of Gates Street, renamed Canton Street, and Upper North Street in Poplar, October 1919. Cardinal Bourne is conducting the service. In the background is St Mary and St Joseph's Catholic Church, which was destroyed in the Blitz.

Introduction

The area now known as the London Borough of Tower Hamlets can be traced back to the Domesday Manor of Stepney, or Stibenhede, an area of approximately 8,144 acres, on the eastern edge of the City of London, with the Thames forming its natural boundary to the south and the River Lea to the east. It included the areas we know as Stepney, Bethnal Green, Poplar and Hackney, as well as the Tower of London. The Manor of Stepney originally consisted of fourteen hamlets – a collection of fishing and farming communities with a total of about 800 inhabitants – although, as the mother parish was subdivided, this increased to twenty-one hamlets. These were what we recognize today as the Tower Hamlets.

Stepney belonged to the Bishopric of London, St Dunstan having held this office in 958–9 AD, and it is to him that the old parish church of Stepney is dedicated. Stepney village life centred around the church of St Dunstan, and the village high street followed the same alignment as that of Stepney High Street. St Dunstan's was the mother church for several hundred years, while chapels of ease such as St Mary's Whitechapel and St Mary's Bow were built for the convenience of worshippers. With the advent of the East India Company in 1603 and the influx of seafarers into Poplar and Blackwall, a petition was made to the company for a chapel. As a result, St Matthias Chapel was built in Poplar in 1654. By 1817, Poplar had become a parish in its own right, when an Act of Parliament allowed for the building of All Saints Church at Newby Place, which was completed in 1823. In Bethnal Green, St Matthew's (built in 1746, rebuilt 1861) became the parish church. The Parish of Stepney thus gradually became fragmented, while the business of the parishes was now conducted in the vestry halls of the Hamlet of Mile End Old Town (Stepney), Limehouse, St George's in the East, Whitechapel, Poplar, Bromley St Leonard's and St Matthew's Bethnal Green. In 1832 the name Tower Hamlets was given to the new parliamentary borough, but with the limited franchise that existed the labouring masses could neither aspire to a seat in the House nor elect one of their own to represent them.

The riverside hamlets have always had strong maritime connections, and the docks along the River Thames have played an important part in the growth and development of a thriving seafaring community. These hamlets were the most populous and, with the increase in maritime trade and the opening of the docks, they attracted ever larger numbers in search of employment.

By the mid-nineteenth century the density of population in the East End of London was causing grave concern, with the wealthier citizens of the city fearful of the spread of disease from the squalor of the slums. Victorian values came into play, large workhouses were built to contain the feckless poor, and Victoria Park was laid out to provide recreation for the general public. This concern for the labouring masses was written about and discussed at great length by Oxford graduates from affluent backgrounds who wished to impart some of their knowledge and values to their less fortunate brethren. Toynbee Hall in Whitechapel was the first university settlement, with Oxford House and a dozen others following shortly after.

The East End of London has traditionally attracted those seeking refuge from oppression and persecution, or those desperately seeking work and a means of earning a livelihood. In the seventeenth century the Huguenots, escaping persecution in France, began to arrive in large numbers, bringing their silk-weaving skills to Spitalfields. The eighteenth century saw an influx of Irish farm workers, who later joined the weaving community and also formed a major part of the workforce during the construction of London's docks. The pogroms in Russia and Poland forced thousands of Jews to flee abroad, and while most saw America as the promised land, London was for many the first port of call. By the end of the nineteenth century the areas in and around Brick Lane became uniquely Jewish in character. Industrious and frugal, the more affluent Jews soon moved to areas such as Golders Green and Stamford Hill in North London. The end of the Second World War saw a new wave of immigration into the East End, as Bengalis, mainly from the Sylheti region, arrived in search of shelter and work. They moved into the semi-derelict warehouses and shops in and around Aldgate and Whitechapel, infusing new life and a new identity into the area.

In 1900, with the huge increase in the population of the East End of London, the area comprising the old Parish of Stepney was carved up to form the metropolitan boroughs of Stepney, Bethnal Green, Poplar, Hackney and Shoreditch. Two world wars later, and with a considerable decline in population, the boundary lines were redrawn yet again, and in 1965, Stepney, Bethnal Green and Poplar merged to form the London Borough of Tower Hamlets. Through all of these realignments of boundaries and changes in names, the inhabitants of Tower Hamlets have clung stubbornly to their own identities. Bethnal Green, Bow, Blackwall, Bromley-by-Bow, the Island, Limehouse, Mile End, Poplar, Ratcliff, Shadwell, Spitalfields, Stepney, Wapping or Whitechapel is where they come from.

Pearly Kings and Queens in the 1920s, during a carnival procession down the East India Dock Road to raise funds for Poplar Hospital. The hospital was damaged during the Second World War, then closed in 1947.

Section One

STEPNEY

An unusual view of St Dunstan's parish church, Stepney, from Spring Garden Place,

c. 1910. The church dates from Saxon times and has the oldest structural foundations in

the East End. On the left, at the junction with Stepney High Street, was No. 38, the Old

Ship, whose licensee in 1910 was Thomas John Newbury. Next door, at No. 2a Spring

Garden Place, was Joseph Wilson, bootmaker. At No. 4 was William Miller, fried fish

dealer. Spring Garden Place is now part of Stepney Way, the buildings have disappeared

and the site forms part of Stepping Stones Farm.

The Anchor and Hope pub, No. 8 Jamaica Street, at the corner of Bermuda Street (now Summercourt Road), 1951, viewed from No. 449 Commercial Road, the premises of Morris Barnett, grocers. The licensee of the Anchor and Hope at this time was John Ellis. Jamaica Street no longer meets Commercial Road, the area having been rebuilt in the 1950s. It is now the Exmouth estate, and No. 449 Commercial Road is part of the Brayford Square Shopping Centre.

Whitechapel Fire Station, *c.* 1910. This early postcard shows the horse-drawn fire engines. The fire station is situated between Manningtree Street and White Church Lane at the western end of Commercial Road, on the north side.

Van No. 195 of the London Co-operative Society (LCS), parked outside a café in Adler Street, 1937. The LCS had its beginnings in the Stratford Co-operative Society (registered in 1861), and by the 1930s was the largest supplier of bread, coal and milk to the housewives of East London.

Workmen clearing up after a particularly heavy bombing raid had left a huge crater in Commercial Road, by Adler Street, 20 April 1941.

Stepney Green, *c.* 1900. This is one of the old village greens that has survived to the present day. Nearby lies Hayfield Passage, a delightful narrow cobbled thoroughfare.

Another view of Stepney Green, *c.* 1900, which shows some of the older weatherboarded houses. Stepney Green, on the south side of Mile End Road, meets Ben Jonson Road at the junction with White Horse Road and Stepney High Street.

The backyard of No. 30 Folgate Street, July 1962. Five families, including seventeen children, lived in this house at that time. Folgate Street joins Shoreditch High Street at Norton Folgate, with Commercial Street forming the third side of the triangle.

Stepney Green Station, Mile End Road, at the corner with Globe Road, 1941. The Whitechapel and Bow Railway, a 2 mile section of the underground system which runs directly under Mile End Road, was completed in 1902. The engineer who designed and constructed the new railway was Cuthbert A. Brereton, whose novel idea for an opening ceremony was a party for a thousand children at the nearby People's Palace.

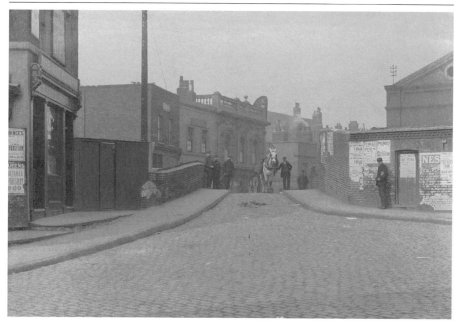

Victory Bridge, over the Regent's Canal, looking west from Rhodeswell Road, 1906. The public house on the left at No. 2 is the Bridge House, whose licensee at this time was Thos. J. Humphreys.

Sidney Square, between Clark Street and Ashfield Street, 1946. These Nissen huts were erected as temporary housing on cleared bomb-damaged sites.

The Edinburgh Castle in Rhodeswell Road at the turn of the century. Once a gin palace and music hall, this property was taken over by Dr Barnardo and converted into a working men's club and people's mission hall. It was opened by Lord Shaftesbury in 1873. Barnardo's left in 1927, and the mission was finally demolished in 1952 to make way for Mile End Stadium.

An accident in Duckett Street, viewed from Ben Jonson Road, looking north-west, 1961. The young lad's pose appears to reflect the policeman's body language. Duckett Street is now part of the Ocean Estate, which incorporates Shandy Park, formerly the site of the old East London Cemetery.

Martineau's sugar factory ruins, *c.* 1884. Mill Yard is in the foreground, where cottages have been cleared for the extension of the London and Blackwall Railway. Martineau Estate, Cable Street, is now on the site.

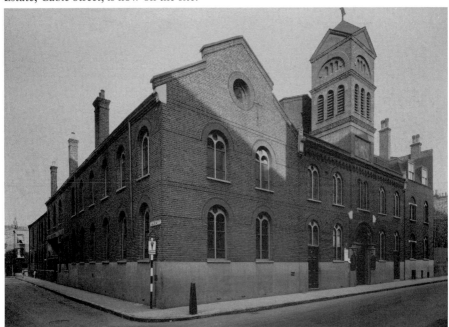

St Boniface German Church and School, Adler Street, 1938. The church was destroyed in the Blitz and has since been replaced by a striking modern building.

Harvest boy statue in Albert Square (now Albert Gardens), Commercial Road, erected by the Metropolitan Public Gardens Association in 1903. This is an example of an early Victorian square, which has retained the original Victorian houses.

The Lycett Hall, East End Mission, Mile End Road, looking south down White Horse Lane. The mission was founded in 1881 by the Methodist Conference. It closed in 1962, and the building was demolished in May 1971. No. 260 is David Cohen, outfitters, on the corner at the junction with White Horse Lane.

A shop on the corner of Fairclough Street and Brunswick Street, next door to Woolsey Bros, cowkeepers, 1938. This shop has an interesting variety of posters advertising tobacco and cigarettes.

A Catholic procession down Commercial Road towards St Mary and St Michael's Catholic Church, from an early postcard. The Vesper and Corner department store was situated at Nos 419–425 Commercial Road, on the north side, on the corner at the junction with Exmouth Street. The store stocked household furniture, carpets and linoleum, and bedding, and it also undertook removals.

The Empire Cinema, Mile End Road, January 1938. The Empire (later the ABC Cinema) stood next to Wickhams department stores. Opposite is Hayfield Passage, which leads to Stepney Green.

Section Two

WAPPING, SHADWELL AND ST GEORGE'S IN THE EAST

Wapping Pier Head, looking west towards Tower Bridge, 1960s.

Tower Bridge from the north-west, 1936. The bridge was opened on 30 June 1894 by the Prince and Princess of Wales. It was designed by Sir Horace Jones, who died before the foundations of the bridge were completed, so the work was finished by George Stevenson. The engineer on the project was Sir John Wolfe Barry. The bridge cost £1,184,000 to build and was paid for by the Bridge House Estates Trust.

The Danish training ship *Danmark* at her berth in Shadwell Basin, 1953. On the left is the steeple of St Paul's Church, Shadwell.

London Docks, *c.* 1890. Wine bottles are being checked in the bonded warehouse.

No. 20 Tower Hill, *c.* 1925. This house is built on the Roman Wall. Nearby is Frederick Jacob & Co., beer merchants. The house has two plaques mounted on the wall. Tower Hill suffered extensive damage during the Second World War.

English Martyrs Catholic Church, Tower Hill. This church is situated on the south side of Prescot Street in Whitechapel. It was designed by Peter Paul Pugin and completed in 1876. It is built in the neo-Perpendicular Gothic style, with a small tower to the left of the entrance. On 29 December 1940 the church was damaged by a high explosive bomb, which failed to explode and was not removed from the floor until 5 February 1941.

The interior of the Cannon Street Road Synagogue, 143 Cannon Street Road, *c.* 1930. The Revd N. Halter is standing on the right. This synagogue belonged to the Federation of Synagogues.

German Lutheran Church of St George, Little Alie Street (now 55 Alie Street), *c.* 1920. The church was built in 1762, through the generosity of Dederick Beckmann, a wealthy sugar-baker, to serve the German community in Whitechapel, many of whom had followed George I to England. The Germans worked for the most part in sugar refineries and bakeries. The adjacent school was founded in 1905.

St George Street (now The Highway), *c.* 1910. The timbered houses are on the corner of Old Gravel Lane, later renamed Wapping Lane.

New Gravel Lane swing-bridge from the north approach, closed for demolition and rebuilding, 1938. The bridge was constructed in 1857 and was in use from early 1858. Approximately 114 feet in length and 17 feet wide, it was lifted for swinging by means of a ram 26½ inches in diameter. New Gravel Lane has been renamed Garnet Street.

St George Street (later The Highway) from Denmark Street looking west towards John's Hill, *c*. 1910.

Ye Olde Globe and Pigeons, 140 High Street, Shadwell, *c*. 1900. No. 134 was The Sun. The High Street was the stretch of road between St George Street or Ratcliff Highway and Broad Street. The entire thoroughfare from East Smithfield – just east of the Tower of London – to the entrance to the Limehouse Link tunnel is now The Highway.

Riverside Mansions, Wapping, 1940, when tenants launched a 'No Rent' strike.

The Riverside Mansions Housing Scheme consisted of six blocks of 163 flats. It was opened in 1928 by Harry Gosling, MP. The mansions overlooked the River Thames and fronted on New Gravel Lane (now Garnet Street).

St George's wash house, Betts Street, early 1960s. This is now part of the swimming pool complex. Mrs Ballard (centre), who was supervisor in the 1960s, is engaged in conversation with Mrs Webbs as she waits for her washing to dry. Note the giant pull-out clothes horses for drying laundry.

The interior of St George's wash house, Betts Street. The street ran between Cable Street and The Highway, in the vicinity of Swedenborg Gardens, and is now reduced to a turning off The Highway. Mrs Webbs is loading her laundry into the washing-machine.

Jamrach's shop in St George Street (now The Highway), boarded up in 1925. Charles Jamrach was an importer and dealer in wild animals of all kinds. Of German origin, he was born in Memel in 1815. He inherited the business from his father, who was an animal dealer in Antwerp and London. When Jamrach died on 6 September 1891, his son took over the running of the business, including the shop in East India Dock Road.

Section Three

LIMEHOUSE AND RATCLIFF

The newly built hostel for British and foreign sailors, opened in 1901, is on the left at the corner of West India Dock Road and Commercial Road. In the distance is St Anne's parish church, one of Nicholas Hawksmoor's three East End churches, which was built in 1723. This postcard view was taken from the junction of East India Dock Road and Burdett Road.

Silver Lion Court entrance, Pennyfields, north side, 1933. Shortly after, the building was demolished under a slum clearance order of 1934. No. 65 is the Silver Lion pub, whose proprietor was Walter Davis, and No. 67 is Tam Wong, a chandler's shop.

Chinese children in Pennyfields, 1932. Most of the children in the area were from mixed marriages between Chinese men, who had settled in Limehouse, and English women.

Ting Kee Refreshments, 39–41 West India Dock Road, 1932. This was the largest and best known Chinese restaurant in Limehouse in the 1930s. It is not listed in the directory after 1942. Next door is the Oporto pub, which is still in business. The buildings to the right were demolished to make way for the extension of the Limehouse police station in 1939. The restaurant has gone, and the gap between the pub and the police station is bridged by a 6-foot high wall.

Padstow Place, Limehouse, just off Three Colt Street, 1932. Note the war memorial mounted on the wall (right). These houses were demolished as part of Stepney Council's slum clearance in 1937–9.

Princess Marie Louise visiting the Gill Street School during a May Festival held in aid of the East London Hospital for Children, 1921.

A horse-drawn sweeper, Narrow Street. These were used by the Stepney Cleaning Depot until 1928. Duke Shore Wharf is in the background, down Duke Shore Alley. To the right at No. 44 is the Barley Mow, whose landlord in 1926 was George Fowler.

Limehouse Church Institute, Three Colt Street, *c.* 1906. Built in 1903, this building was the hall for St Anne's Church, which stood opposite. The institute was refurbished and converted into private apartments in 1989. On the left is the Five Bells and Bladebone pub.

The Catholic Church of Our Lady Immaculate on the south side of Commercial Road, 1950. To the left of the church are Norway Place, Limehouse Library and Norway Wharf, with John Pritchard (Transport) Ltd, R.H. Brookman, builders, and, at No. 642, Mrs Mabel Griffin, dining rooms. The church was built by Father Higley in 1923 and completed in 1934. The library was built in 1901, with half of the cost being provided by the newspaper proprietor John Passmore Edwards. On the right is Island Row and the Convent of the Sisters of Charity of St Vincent de Paul.

Girls surrounding a street seller outside the Freemasons Arms, 96–8 Salmon Lane, *c.* 1920. This Taylor Walker pub is still doing business. Salmon Lane was once the main pathway leading from Limehouse to St Dunstan's Church, and was earlier known as Sermon's Lane.

Nos 10–14 Copenhagen Place, just off Burdett Road, 1938. This row of houses was demolished as part of a slum clearance in 1940–1. The sign on the wall reads: 'No way out'.

Leopold House on the extreme right, and the railway station in Burdett Road, from the south. Leopold House School, for boys aged 10 to 13 years, was one of Dr Barnardo's establishments from 1884. The school closed in March 1908. A tower block, Elmslie Point, now occupies the site. The railway station, on the Great Eastern Railway, opened in 1871. It was damaged during an air raid in December 1940, and closed after a second air raid in April 1941.

The Railway Tavern, later known as Charlie Brown's pub, 1920s. In the centre is the famous Charlie Brown himself, seated with his family and surrounded by some of the thousands of curios he had collected over the years. Brown died in June 1932 and the pub was taken over by his daughter and son-in-law. It was demolished in 1989 to make way for the Limehouse Link road.

Scandinavian Sailors' Temperance Home in Garford Street, a small turning off West India Dock Road, at the turn of the century. This was one of many hostels for seafaring men opened in the East End. The building, and surprisingly the gardens too, are still in existence and the property is owned and run by the Salvation Army as a hostel for men.

Shoulder of Mutton Alley, off Narrow Street on the north side, 1937. Opposite the entrance of the alley is the Bunch of Grapes inn. This is an atmospheric picture of a forgotten corner of Limehouse.

The Empire Memorial Hostel, at the junction of Salmon Lane and Commercial Road, was opened in 1924 as a hostel for sailors. The foundation stone was laid by the Dowager Lady Dimsdale in 1922. The premises have recently been refurbished and converted into luxury apartments.

Public Health Office, No. 43 White Horse Road, August 1937. Formerly the offices of the Board of Works for the Limehouse District, this property was built in 1862. Its exceptionally ornate decorative stonework and wrought-iron lanterns are a fine example of Victorian craftsmanship, and the exterior has retained most of the original features.

The frame of the wooden East Indiaman *Canton*, sunk to form a graving dock by Messrs Fletcher, Son and Fearnall at Union Dock, Limehouse. The *Canton* had made several voyages to India for the East India Company, until it was bought and broken up in 1824. The hull served as a dock until the new Lower Dock was constructed in 1894.

The River Thames at Ratcliff during a severe frost, February 1895. This view is from the causeway of Ratcliff Cross and shows an unusually quiet scene with few ships about. The river has not frozen over completely, but the floating blocks of ice constitute

a hazard to navigation. The Thames has ceased to freeze over since the old London Bridge, whose construction was such that it impeded the flow of water, was removed, and this rare scene is unlikely to be repeated.

The official opening of the Rotherhithe Tunnel by the Prince of Wales, later George V, 12 June 1908. The entrance is in Branch Road, off Commercial Road. The tunnel, linking Ratcliff to Rotherhithe, was designed and constructed by Sir Maurice Fitzmaurice, chief engineer of the London County Council. Its length is 1.3 miles.

AROUND SPITALFIELDS

Children in Crispin Street, outside Spitalfields Market, 1912. This view is from
Brushfield Street, looking south. The costers have stopped to pose, although the boy in the
left foreground appears to be unaware of the photographer.

No. 10 Spital Square, Poltava Synagogue, washed by the rain, *c.* 1920. This building was situated at the north-west corner of Spital Square, on the site of the Priory and Hospital of St Mary Spital. The synagogue was built in 1884 and is listed in the directory of 1920 as the German Synagogue. Off camera to the left is Lamb Street.

Children in Crispin Street, looking towards Brushfield Street, *c.* 1912. The beer retailer at 5 Crispin Street, advertising Charringtons fine ales, was William Ewen. Just within the frame on the left is the Convent of Mercy and the Providence Row night shelter.

Fashion Street Arcade, early 1960s. The Moorish Market was built by Abraham Davis in 1905 as a covered market with sixty-three shops for traders, but it was never popular. Its unusual architecture is still the dominant feature of the street. The shop signs visible in the picture are typical of the area's cultural diversity: J. Minsky (left) and B.S. Saggu (right).

Christ Church Spitalfields, one of Nicholas Hawksmoor's finest churches, which was built between 1714 and 1729. It was left derelict in the 1960s and has since been restored to its former glory. The churchyard (right) was known as Itchy Park when it was the haunt of tramps and the homeless.

St Jude's Church, Commercial Street, being demolished, 1925. The Revd Augustus Barnett was appointed vicar to what was possibly the most underprivileged parish in the East End. In 1884 he founded the adjacent Toynbee Hall, where undergraduates from Oxford were encouraged to spend time educating the working classes. Revd Ernest Carter was a curate here. In 1912 he and his wife, Lily, the sister of social worker Mary Hughes, set sail for America on the ill-fated *Titanic*.

Fournier Street, north side, 1953. No. 15, on the corner of Wilkes Street, with the sign 'The Way', is the Society for the Propagation of the Gospel Among the Jews, and the Gilead Medical Mission. On the left is No. 9, a café run by Mrs Rose Ward, and two doors away at No. 13 was Hyman Rottenberg, hairdresser.

The Original Kosher Wine Company in Osborn Street, which leads into Brick Lane, c. 1900. The sign for the post office is in both English and Russian. The glass-plate negative from which this print was taken has a crack on the left-hand side.

Spring Walk, off Kingward Street, 1955. Before 1938 this was called Spring Gardens, and consisted of a narrow street of cottages built between 1813 and 1819, some of which still survive. Kingward Street was previously known as King Edward Street.

A family in Whitechapel at the turn of the century. This is one of a series of slides taken by the Whitechapel mission, possibly with the intention of using them for fund-raising.

Spital Square, showing posts at the eastern end, 1912. Nos 27 and 28 are immediately on the left. No. 29, a confectioners, is on the right. Church Passage is on the left, with Lamb Street in the distance.

St Mary's mission house, Fieldgate Street, *c*. 1915. A small turning off Whitechapel Road, the street leads directly into Stepney Way. It can be found behind the East London Mosque in Whitechapel Road. The mission house was later a synagogue (1935–*c*. 1950), before becoming a factory and workshop.

The Star Café, No. 15 Commercial Street on the west side, 1955. War-damaged buildings are clearly visible on the left.

Customers at the Star Café. The proprietor was Tabone Bastiana. These two views were taken on 22 September 1955. The premises were demolished in 1957.

Section Five

FROM WHITECHAPEL
TO MILE END

*Queen Alexandra visiting The London Hospital, later Royal London Hospital. The
Queen's association with the hospital began in 1864, when she opened the new Alexandra
ward. Her statue was placed in the nurses' gardens in 1904. The hospital began in 1740
and the buildings in Whitechapel Road opened in 1757.*

St Mary's parish church, Whitechapel, 1870. This church stands on the site of a thirteenth-century 'White Chapel', from which the area took its name. This was replaced by a new building in 1875, which was subsequently destroyed in a fire. The rebuilt church suffered extensive damage in the Second World War, and on 14 July 1945 the spire was struck by lightning, splitting it in two.

St Mary's, Whitechapel, 1910. Bishop Paget opens an event in the garden. This scene of elegance and graciousness took place in the vicinity of Osborn Street and Brick Lane.

Whitechapel Station, 1896. This early photograph shows an array of posters and information regarding trains and destinations. The railway station, which is almost opposite the Royal London Hospital, began in 1869 as part of the East London line. The District Railway Underground station opened on 6 October 1884. On the left, at No. 131, was Daniel Griffin, confectioner.

One of two statues in the courtyard of Trinity Almshouses, 1917. The inscription reads: 'To the memory of Captain Richard Maples (who dying a Commander of a shipp in the East Indies in the year 1680 left to the Trinity House ye value of 1300L with which part of these almeshouses were built) the said Corp. caused this statue to be erected Anno. 1681.'

A view of the east row of cottages in 1917, which together with an identical row on the west side make up Trinity Almshouses, which were built in 1695 on land given by Capt. Henry Mudd for retired merchant seamen. Restored after an impassioned plea by C.R. Ashbee in 1896, they were damaged in the Second World War and restored yet again. Ashbee's interest in the preservation of historic buildings led to his founding The Survey of London.

The Great Assembly Hall, 1899. This property was built by Frederick Charrington, heir to the Charrington Brewery fortune, who turned his back on the family business to spend the rest of his life and wealth promoting temperance. The hall, which was adjacent to Trinity Almshouses, attracted huge audiences, and besides Sunday Services held clubs and meetings for working-class men, women and children.

Whitechapel Bell Foundry, c. 1928. The foundry has been casting bells since Elizabethan times, and the current site dates from 1720. Many of the world's most famous bells, including the Liberty Bell, have been cast or repaired here. Big Ben was recast here after developing a large crack in 1858.

No. 88 Mile End Road, *c.* 1910. This building stood on the south side of the road, not far from Trinity Almshouses, and was the site of the home of James and Elizabeth Cook, during the years when the famous explorer made his discoveries in the South Seas. The house has since been demolished and a plaque erected on a wall at the site. The shopfront of No. 88, Lando, has an interesting display of ladies' corsetry. No. 90 is S. Roseman, bespoke ladies tailor and mantle maker.

Mann Crossman and Paulin, the Albion Brewery, *c.* 1910. The brewery was established in 1760, and covered a wide area, stretching northwards along Cambridge Heath Road. This establishment was closed down by the brewery and part of the site is a new Sainsbury's supermarket. Some of the buildings are being converted into private apartments.

Salvation Army Headquarters, No. 272 Whitechapel Road. This was the Salvation Army's first labour exchange.

Mile End Municipal Baths, 1937. The baths, close to Stepney Green Station, were opened on 12 May 1932 by the Mayor, Cllr Miriam Moses, JP. The facilities on offer were a first-class swimming bath for mixed bathing, first- and second-class slipper baths, foam baths, and Turkish and Russian baths. The baths were later converted into the Globe Centre, which now provides support for AIDS and HIV affected people.

The Vine Tavern, Mile End Road, 1903. A largely wooden house dating from the time of James I, this landmark stood in the middle of the broad pavement near Trinity Almshouses on Mile End Waste. It was bought by Stepney Council in August 1903 and was demolished shortly afterwards.

Mile End Lock, Regent's Canal, viewed from the south, early 1960s. The canal was constructed in the 1830s by John Nash and it is still possible to travel along it from Camden to Limehouse Basin. A scene of tranquillity off the busy highway.

Looking east down Mile End Road, 1934. To the right of the tram is Mile End Station, and to the left is the Plough, a Taylor Walker pub. On the left are the turnings into Frederick Place and Cottage Grove.

Section Six

BETHNAL GREEN

St John's Church, Bethnal Green, c. 1910. This church was designed by Sir John Soane

in 1825. It is surrounded by Bethnal Green Gardens and is situated on the east side of

Cambridge Heath Road, at the intersection with Bethnal Green Road and Roman Road

(previously Green Street).

St Matthew's Church, the oldest church in Bethnal Green, was designed by George Dance in 1746. It has twice been badly damaged: once by fire in 1859 and again during the Second World War. Now restored, it is situated in an oasis of tranquillity off Bethnal Green Road. The old churchyard was laid out as a public garden and opened by the Earl of Meath on 20 July 1897. One of the most controversial curates of St Matthew's was Stewart Headlam, leader of the Christian Socialist Movement.

Oxford House, Derbyshire Street at the corner of Mape Street, *c.* 1900. Mape Street (now also Derbyshire Street) led off from Bethnal Green Road. The mission was founded in 1884 and the impressive Oxford House was opened in 1892. It was one of many university settlements set up in the East End as part of the great philanthropic movement to bring relief and solace to the poverty-stricken masses.

St James the Great Church, Bethnal Green Road, looking towards the north-east, *c.* 1910. This fine red-brick building was constructed in 1844 and now houses private apartments. To encourage the poor to marry rather than simply cohabit, the vicar conducted wedding ceremonies for 6*d*. The market stalls are still a feature of the area.

A clash between Fascists and Communists outside the Salmon and Ball pub, on the corner of Cambridge Heath Road and Bethnal Green Road, 1936. The two rival groups held their meetings on opposite corners of the street.

The men's room at Mildmay Mission Hospital, from an undated slide. The man on the right has a birdcage in front of him, and there appears to be one in the bag hanging on the hook. The notice on the wall reads: 'The buying and selling of wild birds on these premises is an offence and is strictly forbidden.'

The opening of York Hall in Old Ford Road on 5 November 1929 by the Duke and Duchess of York. The hall was built adjacent to the Town Hall and designed along Georgian lines, with red brick, a Portland stone plinth and a cornice. The public baths had first- and second-class swimming baths, washing baths for both sexes, Turkish, electric and vapour baths.

Kitchen staff at Mildmay Mission Hospital, 1930s. Built on its current site in Austin Street, behind Shoreditch Church, in 1892, the mission was set up in Bethnal Green in Turville Street, just off the infamous Old Nichol Street, in response to the dreaded cholera epidemics sweeping the East End of London in the 1860s. Closed in 1982 after being deemed surplus to requirements, the hospital was subsequently reopened in 1985 as an AIDS hospice.

Bethnal Green Infirmary, *c.* 1910. The infirmary was opened on 5 March 1900 on the site of Palestine Place in Cambridge Heath Road. The clock in the tower was a prominent feature of the Palestine Place Chapel and was retained to form a link with the past. Bethnal Green Hospital was under threat of closure in 1989 and was demolished in 1991, to be replaced by a housing complex. The building that housed the School of Nursing is at present still standing.

The Wesleyan Chapel in Approach Road, at the corner with Bonner Road, *c.* 1910.

The London Chest Hospital, Victoria Park, *c.* 1910. This large red-brick building in the Queen Anne style is in Bonner Road. The hospital was founded in 1848 and the present building was opened in 1851. Bishop Bonner's Hall stood to the east of the hospital.

Bethnal Green fire station, Green Street (later Roman Road), from the south, *c.* 1910. The station building now houses the Buddhist Centre, and a new fire station has been built a few yards west along the same road.

The Eagle Slayer, a bronze by John Bell, being erected in front of the Bethnal Green Museum, April 1927. The statue is on the corner of Old Ford Road and Cambridge Heath Road, within the museum grounds. It was removed from the Victoria and Albert Museum and replaced the St George's fountain.

The St George's fountain, Bethnal Green Museum. It was exhibited at the International Exhibition in 1862 and stood in front of the museum from its opening in June 1872 to its demolition in 1926, when it was replaced by the Eagle Slayer. The fountain was in a combination of stone and majolica, by the sculptor J. Thomas, and consisted of 379 separate pieces, forming a structure 30 feet high. The figures of St George and the Dragon are missing from the top.

Bethnal Green Road, looking east from Brick Lane, 1905. On the left is No. 123 Charles Page & Co., cane importers, and the shop next door is Harry Shor & Co., corset makers, then Abraham Rosenberg, tailors. The pub on the right is the Flower Pot, run by William Herbert Harrington Gill.

Oswald Mosley's Blackshirts being moved on, along a road that turns off Green Street (later Roman Road), 30 August 1936. These preliminary displays of Fascism led up to the demonstration on 4 October 1936, when the Great Battle of Cable Street took place.

Gordon Hall Wesleyan Methodist Sunday School, Globe Road, *c.* 1900. Named in honour of General Gordon, the Sunday School was opened in 1885 and was part of the East End mission. It closed in 1958.

Palestine Place, Episcopal Jews' Chapel and London Jews' Society's School, Cambridge Road (later Cambridge Heath Road), *c.* 1880. The Operative Jewish Converts' Institute is on the right. Palestine Place was built in 1814, and was the first place of worship in England for Christian Jews, and for the conversion of Jews to Christianity. Bethnal Green Infirmary was later built on the site.

Columbia Road School, 1915. This was one of the first four feeding centres opened to alleviate the suffering and hardship of families who were left to starve while the men were away on the battle front.

Laying the foundation stone, St Barnabas's Church, 1865. This is one of the earliest photographs in the collection at Bancroft Library. The church stands at the north-east corner of the junction of Grove Road and Roman Road. Damaged during the Second World War, the building was repaired but no longer has a spire.

Section Seven

POPLAR

St Matthias's Church, Poplar Recreation Ground, winter 1935. Built as the East India Company Chapel in 1654, this church was renovated in 1776 and major alterations were made in 1876. The church was closed in 1976 and is now used as a community centre.

All Saints Parish Church and churchyard, Newby Place, *c.* 1920. The architect was Charles Hollis. The church was built in 1823 with a loan from George Green, shipbuilder and philanthropist of Poplar, following a petition from the people of Poplar for their own parish, which was granted in 1817. The land was the gift of Mrs Ann Newby, who also bequeathed her house for use as the vicarage. The house was not considered suitable and was replaced with the present elegant three-storey rectory opposite the church.

Commemorative arch in East India Dock Road, 1897. This was erected in celebration of the 80th anniversary of All Saints parish. When the hamlet of Poplar and Blackwall was created a separate parish in 1817, a mace was made for the vestry of All Saints. The head of the mace was a replica in silver of the West India Dock Gate, and the arch that straddled the road was also a replica of the gate.

All Saints' bells ready for rehanging, after being retuned, 1926. The bells had been silent since 1915.

The Poplar Hospital for Accidents, with the East India Dock Gates on the right. This hospital was opened to deal with the increasing number of accidents and injuries that occurred in the docks. The first patient was Elhmann Rowland, who was admitted with severe injuries on 23 July 1855. The buildings were damaged during the Blitz and the hospital closed in 1976 due to lack of funds for repair work. Demolished in 1981–2, all that remains of this Poplar landmark is a tall chimney.

The demolition of the East India Dock wall, when this section of the road was being widened, August 1912. The new wall is on the left. The dock gates and the tower (right) were demolished in 1959 and a plaque placed in the wall. This wall was demolished when the import dock was filled in and the *Financial Times* building was erected on the site.

Beating the bounds of All Saints Parish, this fine group of parishioners is posing outside the entrance to Poplar Town Hall, Newby Place, opposite All Saints Church.

St Leonard's Road on the corner of Drew Street, 1956. J. Halls and Son, haulage contractors, are on the right, and in the distance is the Hearts of Oak pub. All of this and much more was swept away to build the northern approach to the Blackwall Tunnel, which was opened in 1962.

Unveiling the anchor at Poplar Recreation Ground, July 1911. The anchor was from the royal yacht, *Victoria and Albert*, and was placed on a plinth surrounded by a flower-bed. The anchor was removed during the Second World War, presumably for scrap.

The 'Old English fair' at Poplar Recreation Ground, September 1919. The fair was organized by the Mayor, Revd William Lax, as a peace celebration. To the right is the bandstand. The children in the foreground are in marked contrast to the children below.

Hale Street, adjacent to Poplar Recreation Ground. This photograph was taken at the same time as the one above. These are the children of the fairground folk, preparing their dinner outside their caravan.

East India Dock Road in 1959, when work on the second Blackwall Tunnel was under way, after removal of the dock entrance and the Blackwall Tunnel entrance. The entire row of buildings in the background – from Robin Hood Lane to Cotton Street, including the Beehive in the centre, the Poplar Palais and the pub – has been demolished to widen the road yet again, work which took at least 5 years.

East India Dock Road, Nos 235–43 on the north side, c. 1926. No. 237 was Whiffin's Studios. William Whiffin was a prolific photographer, and it is thanks to him that we have such a useful photographic record of Poplar, especially from the Second World War. Bottoms & Co., at 241 East India Dock Road, appears to sell everything from Benledi cycles to gramophones and wireless sets.

Board of Trade Offices, East India Dock Road. Originally a sailors' home, these premises were built by George Green and supported later by his son Richard. Green's Home was very costly to run, and was later used as the offices for the Board of Trade, where ships' crews signed on. An elegant building that survived the Second World War, it has been converted into flats and is run by the Rodinglea Housing Association.

Poplar Baths was one of the first public baths and wash houses to be erected in London, in 1856. This early photograph shows the original building. The baths that replaced it on this site, built in 1933, were closed in 1987 and the building was converted into a Youth Training Workshop.

Women in Poplar Workhouse with the matron, *c.* 1900. The workhouse on Poplar High Street was feared by the poor, and its spartan regime included the separation of husband and wife, and of mother and child. It was demolished in 1960 and Tower Hamlets College was built on part of the site. Stoneyard Lane ran along the west side.

Richard Green's statue, erected in 1866 outside Poplar Baths, East India Dock Road. The only surviving son of George Green from his first marriage, Richard joined his father's shipbuilding firm at Blackwall and constructed some of the most famous East Indiamen. Here he is seen seated on a chair covered by a sail-cloth, with his faithful dog, Hector. On the sides of the plinth are two fine bas-reliefs of Blackwall Yard. In the background is King George's Hall, on the corner of Bath Street. This was originally Bath Street Chapel, one of the earliest Wesleyan chapels in London.

Poplar Methodist Church, known universally as Lax's Church, on the corner of East India Dock Road and Woodstock Road, now Woodstock Terrace, 1925. The latter name derives from Edward Wood Stock, a landowner in Poplar, whose grandfather ran the Academy for Gentlemen in Poplar High Street.

Lax's new church, newly refurbished, at the opening ceremony, Saturday 30 September 1933. Revd William Lax toured the world, raising funds for his church in the East India Dock Road.

The Sisterhood at Lax's Church, which numbered 1,200, was organized by Mrs Minnie Lax, sometimes referred to by her admirers as the 'Mother of Poplar'. She was a familiar sight on Sundays, when she played her harmonium and sang hymns to gather the crowds at the dock gates before the Revd Lax delivered his hour-long sermons.

Bow Common Lane Bridge, looking north from Upper North Street. Popularly known as 'Stink House Bridge', it was built c. 1780 over Limehouse Cut, which was constructed in 1770. Several factories manufacturing chemical products such as vitriol, varnish, pitch, naphtha and animal charcoal were set up on either side of the Cut shortly after it was opened, and the waterway that connects the Lea with the River Thames was soon heavily polluted by noxious effluents, hence the name. The bridge was closed on 4 May 1927 and rebuilt. The road, which becomes Bow Common Lane, follows the line of the ancient pathway from Poplar High Street to Bow Common.

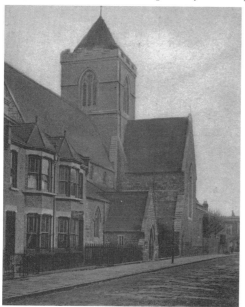

St Mary and St Joseph's Catholic Church, looking east down Gates Street (now Canton Street) towards Upper North Street, c. 1910. This church was built in 1856 and was demolished by a land mine on 8 December 1940. Blessed John Roche School was built on the site, and the high altar is marked by a mound surmounted by a large crucifix. The new church, built in 1954 on the opposite side, is on the corner of Canton Street and Upper North Street.

St Mary and St Joseph's Catholic Church, Gates Street (later Canton Street). This rare view of the interior of the church shows the high altar, under which lay the remains of Father Benjamin Barber, the first parish priest, who came to Poplar in 1817 to set up a chapel and school in Wade's Place, at the request of the Irish Catholic dockworkers.

Old Cottages in Poplar, a view of the backyard, c. 1930. Great damage was inflicted on Poplar during the Second World War, and in 1951 large areas of the district were completely cleared to make way for the Lansbury Estate, the live architectural exhibition of the Festival of Britain.

Offices of Walter Windrum, Son & Trimming, auctioneers and estate agents, at 172 East India Dock Road, south side, *c.* 1937.

Two children examining a car outside H. Lyons, tailors, 180 East India Dock Road, 1924. This charming scene was captured on camera by William Whiffin from the upstairs window of his photographic studios.

Nos 176–180 East India Dock Road. Dr Skelly, seen waving his umbrella, lived at No. 178 for many years and died there on 19 August 1932. At the extreme left, at 180 East India Dock Road, is the establishment of H. Lyons, tailor.

The last service in St Stephen's Church, held in the ruins on VE Day, 8 May 1945. Revd H.L. Evans, Vicar of St Matthias's, took the service. The church stood on the corner of East India Dock Road and Upper North Street and was consecrated in 1867. The site was later cleared for the Festival of Britain Exhibition in 1951. A stone wall along East India Dock Road was built from the rubble.

HRH Princess Margaret opens the new St Nicholas and All Hallows Church Hall, Aberfeldy Street, Saturday 22 October 1955. The church was built to replace All Hallows' Church, East India Dock Road, and St Nicholas Church, Blackwall, both of which were destroyed during the Blitz. On the left of the Princess is prebendary Mark Hodson, Rector of All Saints, Poplar (later Bishop of Hereford).

Section Eight

BOW AND
BROMLEY-BY-BOW

Coborn School, Bow Road, looking north-east, c. 1910. This school for girls was established after a bequest from Prisca Coborn (or Coburne), who died in 1701. It was originally situated behind St Mary's Church, Bow. In 1814 a new school was opened in Fairfield Road, and in 1892 it moved into the vacated old Coopers' Company School for Boys at No. 86 Bow Road. In 1973 Coborn School and Coopers' Company School moved to Upminster.

Harley College, Bow Road, looking north-west at the turn of the century. Harley College was the headquarters of the Regions Beyond Missionary Union where medical missionaries were trained for service in Africa and the Far East. The milestone in the foreground is still in place and can be found close to Electric House.

Bow County Court, an early postcard view. This building, situated on the south side of Bow Road, was demolished and replaced by the Thames Magistrates' Court.

The City of London Institution, Bow Road, 1905. This is the dreaded workhouse, the buildings of which were converted in 1912 to the Bow Infirmary for the honest, aged poor. Now St Clement's, it is the psychiatric unit of the Royal London Hospital.

Harley College Grounds, *c.* 1910. The Phoenix Open Air School was later built on these grounds.

Paper boys posing in Roman Road, Bow, at the eastern end, early 1900s. On the right is 114 Roman Road, the shop of Lewis Brothers, pawnbrokers, at the corner of Medway Road. Now No. 384, the premises are occupied by Harbuds furnishers. Further along is Charles Terrace. The shops and buildings along this section of the road have survived virtually unscathed and this view is easily identifiable.

Malmesbury Road School, c. 1920, celebrating Empire Day, which was held annually on 24 May. A piano draped with the Union flag has been wheeled into the playground, and it was customary for the girls to dress in white with ribbons of red, white and blue. After the singing of 'Land of Hope and Glory', the school would have a half-holiday.

May Day procession, Old Ford Road, viewed from the top of 400 Old Ford Road, the Women's Hall, 24 May 1914. Sylvia Pankhurst is leading the contingent of women from the East London Federation of the Suffragettes to Victoria Park. The pub next door, just visible on the extreme right, is the Lord Morpeth. The curved factory building in the background is in a state of serious disrepair today.

Unveiling the memorial clock to the late Edward W. McCullum, JP, at Bow Library, Roman Road, 16 May 1917. McCullum was a local boy, having been born in Bethnal Green, lived in Bow and attended Fairfield Road School. He was a well-known philanthropic worker who died in 1914.

This arch was the entrance to the old Northumberland House, Whitehall, which was demolished in 1823. The arch was re-erected in the grounds of Tudor House in St Leonard's Street, now the site of the Bromley Recreation Grounds, known locally as Bob's Park. The two statues at the foot of the arch disappeared some time in the 1940s. A £4 million health centre and park development scheme is currently under way on the site.

The statue of William Gladstone, in mourning because of the death nine days earlier of the great statesman, 28 May 1898. This was erected in 1882 by William Bryant, of the Bryant and May match factory, who was a staunch admirer of the Liberal prime minister. In the background is St Mary's Church, Bow, which dates back to the fourteenth century. It has been rebuilt and repaired over the centuries, most recently after the tower was extensively damaged during the Second World War.

St Mary's Church, Bromley St Leonard's, 1926. All that remains of this medieval church is the How Memorial Gateway, which was opened on 30 June 1894 to honour the Revd George How, who was the vicar for 20 years. Part of the churchyard is now the St Leonard's Adventure Playground. The rest of the grounds, including the site of the church, has been swallowed up by the northern approach to the Blackwall Tunnel. The church was originally the chapel of the Priory of St Leonard's, founded in the eleventh century at Stratford-atte-Bowe.

St Andrew's Hospital, Devon's Road, *c.* 1934. This hospital was opened in 1871 as the Poplar and Stepney Sick Asylum for workhouse inmates requiring medical attention. It was built at a cost of £43,000, with an additional £7,300 for the site. The architects were Arthur and C. Harston of Poplar. St Andrew's is now part of Newham Health Authority.

Limehouse Cut, looking west from the St Leonard's Street area, 1956. The flats on the left are Brushwood House and Irvine House. In the distance is the railway bridge that now carries the Docklands Light Railway to Stratford.

The gas works at Twelvetrees Crescent, Bromley-by-Bow, an aerial view from the inter-war years. In the foreground the River Lea curves round to become Bow Creek. The bridge in the distance takes Twelvetrees Crescent over to join Gillender Street. This

extensive site, the head office of the gas company, houses a gas museum and depot for spares. A conservation area, it has recently been put forward by the boroughs of Newham and Tower Hamlets as a site for the millennium celebrations.

Bow Brewery, Bromley High Street, by Bow Bridge, demolished in 1933 to make way for Bradley House, a block of flats built by the London County Council. The brewery, Smith and Garretts, had been in existence for a number of years prior to being rebuilt in 1821.

Bow Bridge, north side, *c.* 1912. The premises on the right are those of J.W. French and Co., millers. Smith and Garretts, brewers, are in the distance. Traditionally, the story is that the bridge was built with an arch or bow over the River Lea in the late eleventh century, at the behest of Queen Mathilda, after she and her retinue narrowly escaped drowning while fording the river on their way to Barking Abbey. The bridge has been rebuilt several times over the centuries and is now the site of the Bow flyover.

The Royal College of St Katharine, Maternity and Child Welfare Centre, Brunswick Road, *c.* 1935. This road is now part of the Northern Approach to the Blackwall Tunnel. The building to the right of the hospital is the Bromley Library, now closed and in a sad state of disrepair.

The old Mitford Bridge, Wick Lane, 1926. This bridge was built in the early 1800s. The Mitford Castle public house, which opened for business in 1894, is in the centre of the picture.

The new Mitford Bridge, which replaced the old one in 1927, c. 1946. The bridge crosses Duckett's Canal, which runs alongside Victoria Park. In the background is St Mark's Church, and to the left is W. Myers and Sons Ltd, timber merchants.

People taking the air by the boating lake in Victoria Park, *c.* 1930. The park was designed by James Pennethorne, who began work in 1842. It was in use from about 1845 and proved to be very popular with the working classes. The boating lake had boats for hire, and a large rowing-boat ferried children around the islands. In the background is the boathouse and refreshment saloon.

The ceremony of beating the bounds, Bromley St Leonard's, *c.* 1882. This event took place on the River Lea, with the Revd George How, Vicar of St Mary's Church, Bromley St Leonard's, officiating.

Victoria Park drinking fountain, 1930. Built at a cost of £5,000 in 1862, the drinking fountain was the gift of Angela Burdett-Coutts to the people of the East End. The architect was H.A. Darbishire and the style is everything from French cathedral and chateau to thirteenth-century Gothic. It served a valuable purpose, however, in providing clean drinking water at a time when cholera was rife. The structure has recently been refurbished and is now railed off and inaccessible to the public.

Section Nine
THE ISLE OF DOGS
AND BLACKWALL

The Antarctic ship Endurance *at the entrance to the West India Docks, 1914. This
ship, originally the* Polaris, *was purchased by Sir Ernest Shackleton in 1914 to
accompany his Imperial TransAntarctic expedition. In January 1915, while in the
Antarctic, she was trapped in the ice of the Weddell Sea. The ship was abandoned and
finally sank in November 1915.*

The entrance to the Blackwall Tunnel, opened in 1897, with a view of Tunnel Gardens (left). The gardens were an oasis of greenery in this densely populated corner of Poplar, and they were very popular with children. Both the entrance arch and the gardens were demolished to make way for the second tunnel, which was opened in 1967.

Building Blackwall Tunnel, the final stages. The construction of the tunnel was one of the engineering feats of the late nineteenth century. It was undertaken by Sir Weetman Pearson, who had successfully constructed a tunnel under the Hudson River in New York.

Millwall Dock Hotel, No. 233 West Ferry Road, *c*. 1910. The licensee at this time was William Samuel Innocent Lewis. The pub was next door to the Seamen's Institute. In 1941, the last time the premises were listed in the directory, it was called the Millwall Dock Tavern and the licensee was Mrs Olive Sophie Nayler. The site is now derelict land, and the terraced row alongside begins with 237 West Ferry Road.

Caught by a 'bridger' at the entrance to the West India Docks, probably 1920s. All traffic came to a halt once the bridge was raised to allow ships to pass through into the docks. Although not a frequent occurrence, the Blue Bridge is occasionally raised to let river traffic in and out of the docks.

Blackwall Reach, the River Thames, 1949. Small craft of all description create a scene of busy industry on the river. Sadly, much of this is now a distant memory.

Charrington, Gardner and Locket's new Poplar oil depot at Blackwall, looking north-west, 1959. In the background on the left is the London County Council block of flats, Alberta House, and further along is the Brunswick Arms. The depot closed in 1987 and the site has been left derelict.

A plaque erected at Blackwall as a memorial to the Virginia settlers, who set sail from Blackwall Stairs in December 1606 in three ships, the *Susan Constant*, the *Discovery* and the *Godspeed*. Capt. John Smith headed the group of 105 adventurers, the first permanent settlers in America. Governor Stanley of Virginia stands beside the granite monument during a commemorative service held on 12 October 1956.

The launch of HMS *Sans Pareil* from the Thames Iron Works and Shipbuilding Company at Orchard House Yard, 9 May 1887. Thomas Ditchburn and C.J. Mare established the first iron shipyard at Blackwall in 1834, and within the next ten years, hundreds of the fastest steam ships, yachts and boats were launched. On 21 June 1898, during the launch of HMS *Albion*, thirty-eight spectators were killed when the slipway was smashed by a massive wave as the ship entered the water.

The Yarrow and Hedley shipbuilding works on the Isle of Dogs, *c.* 1870. This is a view of the original yard, which was situated next to the Folly House on Folly Wall, in Stewart Street, south of the entrance to the West India Docks. Shipbuilding began here in 1866 and continued on the site until Yarrow (the partnership ended in 1875) moved to Glasgow soon after it launched its last ship in the River Thames, a Dreadnought, in 1908.

Yarrow's Boat Yard, July 1886. This is one of the twenty-three torpedo boats built for the Government by Yarrow and Co. It measured 125 feet in length and its beam was 13 feet. Yarrow's built its first torpedo boat in 1877 and its first torpedo boat destroyer in 1892.

Island Gardens at the southern end of the Isle of Dogs. On the left is the entrance to the Greenwich Foot Tunnel, opened in 1902, which provides pedestrian access across the River Thames. The gardens were financed by the London County Council and opened by Will Crooks, MP, in 1895.

Small craft on the River Thames. This nostalgic scene dates back to the days when river craft of all descriptions were a familiar sight in Blackwall Reach.

One of the eights at the Poplar, Blackwall and District Rowing Club's Regatta on the River Thames, 6 October 1963. The clubhouse was built alongside the entrance to the Greenwich Foot Tunnel on the site of the North Greenwich Station, which was demolished after the Second World War. Across the river is the *Cutty Sark*, now a museum ship, once the fastest tea clipper to sail the route to China carrying her precious cargoes of tea. The ship made eight trips in all for her owner, John 'Old White Hat' Willis.

Canadian troops who disembarked at Millwall Docks march down West Ferry Road on their way to London for the coronation of George V, held on 22 June 1911. The building on the extreme right is St Luke's School, opposite Strafford Street.

A dock constable frisking a suspect at the West India Docks. Workers leaving the docks were routinely checked for stolen goods.

Robert Milligan's statue at the entrance to the West India Docks, 1899. Milligan was the promoter and first Deputy Chairman of the West India Dock Company. West India Dock Gate was demolished in 1932. The sugar warehouses in the background were severely damaged during the Blitz. Those remaining are being refurbished and will house the Museum in Docklands, where hopefully the statue will be on display.

Section Ten

EAST END MARKETS

Petticoat Lane Market at the turn of the century. Although renamed Middlesex Street, this
road has persistently refused to alter its traditional name. It is still one of London's best
known street markets and is very popular with tourists. It has spread into several
sidestreets around Spitalfields.

The cycle market in Club Row, Bethnal Green, *c.* 1910. Going 'down the Row' was one way of spending a pleasant Sunday morning. Club Row connected the new London County Council Boundary Estate in the north with Bethnal Green Road and nearby Bishopsgate Goods Station of the Great Eastern Railway in the south. It was at one time linked to Sclater Street, from which it became isolated when Bethnal Green Road was extended in 1879.

Lamb Street and the Flower Market at Spitalfields, on the corner of the junction with Commercial Street, 1912. Hintons was one of the larger merchants. The building was very recently gutted by a fierce blaze.

An interior view of Spitalfields Market, 1912. The costers' wicker baskets are stacked high on the shelves, and crates of fruit and vegetables are on the extreme left. The market dates back to 1685. In 1928 new market buildings occupying over 5 acres were opened by Queen Mary. A new purpose-built complex has been constructed at Temple Mills and the old buildings are now put to good use as a Sunday arts and crafts, health food and antiques fair.

Harrow Place, Petticoat Lane Sunday Market, August 1958. The auctioneer's 'plant' or stooge encourages potential buyers to part with their money. Harrow Place is a small turning off the west side of Middlesex Street, connecting with Cutler Street and White Kennet Street.

A stallholder in Petticoat Lane (Middlesex Street), just one of the many characters who make this market so popular with tourists, August 1958.

Beigel sellers around Brick Lane, c. 1900. This was a welcome sight well into the 1940s. The familiar cry of 'beigel, beigel, beigel' from the beigel woman would bring East End children out with their pennies.

Looking over clothes in Brick Lane at the turn of the century. The women's clothes strongly suggest their middle European origins. Many East End families could not afford new clothes and made do with second-hand garments from street stalls.

'The Ghetto, London' is the caption on this early postcard of c. 1900. This is a reference to the large numbers of Russian and Polish Jews who had sought refuge in the Brick Lane area. The man in the left foreground is wearing what looks like a pith helmet or solar topee.

Columbia Market being demolished, 1960. This magnificent Gothic structure was the gift of Baroness Angela Burdett-Coutts, the great Victorian heiress and philanthropist. The architect was Henry Darbishire. The market was intended to replace the street markets and provide a place where costers could trade under cover. However, the traders stubbornly refused to use the building, preferring their traditional pitches. Partially damaged during the Second World War, the market lay derelict before being demolished by the Greater London Council.

Randall's Market, looking west towards Upper North Street, 1920s. The market never really took off, and consisted mainly of lock-up shops selling second-hand goods. There were a number of statues decorating the market; the one which graced the Horn of Plenty pub was found in the rubble when the market was demolished in the 1950s. It was mounted on a plinth on the wall of the new Susan Lawrence School in Cordelia Street. The shops in the background are No. 47, C. Kind, beer retailer; No. 49, Thomas E. Haynes, coffee rooms; and No. 51, Joseph Lisek, hairdresser.

Chrisp Street Market viewed from East India Dock Road with Barclays Bank on the left, 1937. Outside the bank stood Burgess's fruit and vegetable stall. Next to the bank was the eel shop and then the Star in the East, a public house. Barclays Bank has moved a short distance to the corner of Kerbey Street.

Chrisp Street Market from the corner of Grundy Street, looking north, November 1950. This is one of the last photographs of the market before its removal to the new Lansbury housing estate, which was completed after the Festival of Britain in 1951.

A man selling puppies in Club Row, off Bethnal Green Road, c. 1925. Club Row was established as a bird fair by the 1850s and, with the neighbouring Sclater Street, was also a noted market for small animals (including stolen dogs). The row is a quiet and sedate thoroughfare today.

Section Eleven
TRANSPORT

Stepney Council refuse vehicles lined up, from the horse-drawn cart to the most up-to-date

lorry, 1930s.

Firemen tackling a blaze at the Cotton Street Baptist Chapel, 23 May 1914. The chapel was on the east side of Cotton Street, which runs south from East India Dock Road to Poplar High Street. The area was devastated in March 1945 by a V2 rocket, which landed on the corner of Bazely Street and East India Dock Road.

The no. 23 bus, East Ham to Marylebone, 1923. This bus route existed until *c*. 1985, when London Transport rationalized its bus routes.

Poplar Borough Council book salvage bus, *c*. 1940. Several of the posters plastered all over the bus read: 'Bring your books here'. Others read: 'The Nation needs your books', 'We want your kitchen waste', 'Rags for salvage', 'Save wastepaper', and 'Salvage saves shipping'.

A horse-drawn tramcar belonging to the North Metropolitan Company, 1879. The sign on the side reads: 'Elephant & Castle Horse Repository, New Kent Road'; and below that: 'Moorgate St, Old St, Hackney Road and Clapton'.

London General omnibus, route no. 23, which travelled from East Ham down the East India Dock Road and Commercial Road, 1923. The *Evening Standard*, advertised along the side of the vehicle, is still one of London's most popular newspapers.

North London Railway Station in the Bow Road, north side, 1930. The station opened
in 1870 and closed in 1944. It was finally demolished in 1975. The Bow and Bromley
Institute had its premises above the station. The ornate drinking fountain in the centre
was erected by subscription from the Bryant and May match factory workers, who were
docked 1s a week from their wages to pay for it. (The average weekly wage was
between 4s and 8s, equivalent to 20p to 40p.) The fountain commemorated the defeat
of the proposed bill to levy a match tax. It was demolished in April 1953 when Bow
Road was widened.

The Empress no. 8 bus route from Old Ford to Edgware Road, via Oxford Street. This route is still in existence, running from Bow Church to Victoria Station.

Cricketers Bridge, Old Ford Road, 1937. A canal barge negotiates the narrow arch on the Regent's Canal, while a group of children watch with interest. The building in the background, once Bowbrook School, was converted in the 1970s into private apartments.

Old Ford Lock on the Regent's Canal, Victoria Park, 1933. This is a charming scene of tranquillity in the heart of the East End.

Great Eastern Railway Bridge, Old Ford Road, 1950. This bridge was built in 1836 and was widened twice: in 1845 and 1890. The man on the back of the vehicle appears to be leaning out to check if the lorry has sufficient clearance.

A horse-drawn dustcart, 1951. These carts were in use until 1952 for general work on highways, for carting away materials, picking up rubbish, etc. The horses were hired from H. Green and Son, Rifle Street, Poplar.

Section Twelve
WORKING LIFE

Waste disposal on the River Thames, 1949. The two workers are levelling off the refuse in the barge prior to hatching and covering it for the trip down river. This was a most unpleasant task, and offered scant regard for safety.

The Whitechapel Bell Foundry, on the corner of Whitechapel Road and Plumbers Row, 1916. The foundry was established in Elizabethan times and has been casting and repairing bells ever since.

Women at spinning-wheels, 1908. Silk weaving was already a dying art when this picture was taken. The weavers of Spitalfields were descendants of the Huguenots who arrived in England in large numbers towards the end of the seventeenth century. The last of the weavers lived and worked in Bethnal Green until the 1930s. Remnants of the last surviving looms can be found in Braintree and Bocking, Essex.

John Sayers, cooperage, 33a Ropery Street, Bow, c. 1930. This business commenced in 1881 and closed in 1957. John Charles Sayers is the small boy in the centre; the foreman, Jim Ramsey, is in the background wearing a trilby; on his right is Jack Dowell; and in the front row, second from the left, is Charles Edward Sayers. Harry Bethal and Tim Bell are also present. The making of barrels was a highly skilled trade, and much sought after, especially in the docks.

A shoeshine boy at work on Gardiner's Corner, July 1909. This corner of Whitechapel Road and Commercial Road has lost many of its distinctive buildings. The old soldier on the left proudly wears his medals.

This photograph of women workers in a factory making army uniforms was taken during the First World War in Sugar Loaf Walk, a small turning between Victoria Park Square and Globe Road, behind the Bethnal Green Museum. On the extreme left is Elizabeth Coe, and next to her standing in full view is her sister Ethel. Women, who were employed to replace men who had been sent to the front, often worked a 16 hour day, 7 days a week.

Devine & Co, whalebone cutters, on the north side of Wright's Road, *c.* 1910. This factory, established in 1880, was on the corner of St Stephen's Road, Bow, opposite St Paul's Church. Whalebone was used for stiffening garments and was an essential part of women's corsetry. The man on the left is watching the dog intently, ready to grab hold of it should it move. At present, an extension to Old Ford School is being built in Wright's Road, and the nursery playground will be on the site of the factory.

The tailors' hiring fair on a Sunday morning at Whitechapel, 1964.

Day's Bird Cage Shop, No. 198 Cambridge Road (later Cambridge Heath Road), 1905. A sign in the window reads: 'Budgies boarded during your holidays.' The shop, on the corner of Patriot Square, was not listed in the directory after 1908. Mayfield House is now on part of the site.

An East End family making streamers, an occupation that appears to have involved the whole family and taken up most of their home. Women and children worked long hours at matchbox making, sewing, sackmaking, brushmaking, etc. for paltry wages.

Brothertons, ironmongers, 566 Commercial Road, south side, 1910. This shop is still selling the same sort of goods – pots and pans, wire and sheet metal work – as it did at the turn of the century. No. 566 is very close to Limehouse Station, previously Stepney East, part of the Docklands Light Railway.

Nos 8–26 Stepney Causeway, Dr Barnardo's Homes, in the bootmaking workshop. From the age of thirteen, young boys were taught trades such as bootmaking, carpentry and tailoring. Others were shipped to the colonies to work on farms.

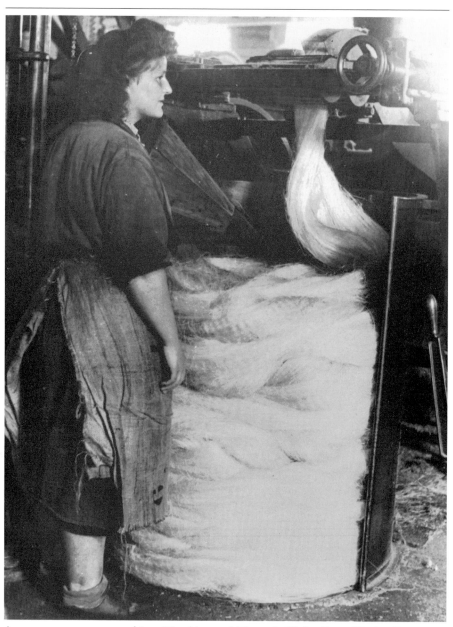

A young woman ropemaking, Hawkins and Tipson's Globe Rope Works, East Ferry Road, Millwall. The rope works was established in 1881 and produced ropes of all sizes. The firm closed in 1971.

Section Thirteen
PEOPLE AND PLACES

From Poplar Town Hall to Holloway Prison, the five women on Poplar Council are

cheered on their way down East India Dock Road, September 1921. From right to left are

Nellie Cressall, mother of five and seven months pregnant, Susan Lawrence, Julia Scurr,

Jennie Mackay and Minnie Lansbury, who was the daughter-in-law of George Lansbury,

leader of the Poplar Rates Dispute. When Labour came to power in Poplar in 1919, one

of the first actions was to refuse to collect the rates, which were one of the highest of all the

London boroughs.

Will Crooks (left) and Elizabeth, his wife, 1919. They are seeing off the five hundred Poplar boys and girls who were being taken on a trip to Epping Forest. This outing was organized by the Poplar Branch of the National Federation of Discharged Sailors and Soldiers. Will Crooks, MP for North Woolwich, was born in Poplar and lived all his life there. He was admired and respected by people in all walks of life for his integrity and honesty. He was very ill at the time this picture was taken and died two years later.

The Bow and Bromley Talmud Torah celebrates Jewish New Year at the Mile End Palladium, September 1922. The Palladium was at 370 Mile End Road, on the south side, opposite Bancroft Road. It was destroyed in the Blitz and the area was cleared in the mid-1950s for the Ocean Estate.

Muriel Lester being greeted by the Mayor of Poplar, Cllr J. Gillender, at her 80th birthday party, Monday 9 December 1963. Muriel Lester and her sister Doris worked among the people of Bromley-by-Bow for many years. They founded Kingsley Hall in Bruce Road, and while Doris continued her work with children, Muriel travelled the world, working tirelessly for peace and reconciliation. A friend of Mahatma Gandhi, who stayed at Kingsley Hall in 1934, she was honoured and revered the world over.

Sister Esther's sewing circle at the Bromley by Bow Baptist Tabernacle. Sister Esther Thynne (standing, left) was a deaconess at the 'Tab' and helped to organize the women's groups and the Sunday School. When the tabernacle was destroyed on 7 September 1940, Sister Esther set up a chapel in the Old Five Bells Temperance Pub in St Leonard's Street, where she organized the Sunday Services, the Baptist minister having retired to Brighton.

Nellie Cressall being presented with the Freedom of the Borough on Wednesday 8 April 1959. She was the first woman to be so honoured. She is seen here with the Mayor of Poplar, Cllr E.H. Smith, the former Labour prime minister Clement Attlee and Mrs Violet Attlee. Nellie Cressall joined Sylvia Pankhurst and the East London Federation of the Suffragettes in Bow, and she had a close friendship with Sylvia. Nellie was a Poplar councillor from 1919 to 1965, and Mayor in 1943/4. She was one of the councillors sent to prison during the Poplar Rates Dispute. She died in 1973 at the age of eighty-one.

Fern Street, off Devon's Road, looking north, with the Fern Street Settlement in the background. The little girl on the right steps through the arch and is handed her farthing bundle. The inscription over the arch reads: 'Enter all ye children small, none can come who are too tall.' Clara Grant, head teacher of the Devon's Road Infants School for twenty-five years, started the settlement in 1907, inspired by the work done at Toynbee Hall. One of the most popular events at Fern Street was the distribution on Saturdays of farthing bundles of oddments that were handed out to the children. The little wooden arch was created in order to limit the numbers who turned up in the hope of collecting a bundle.

Singapore Sam, a charming picture taken at the Chinese Mission in Pennyfields. Intriguingly, there are some Chinese characters penned on the reverse of this picture.

Chinese children at the Chun Yee Chinese Sunday School in Pennyfields, 1950s. The Sunday School and the Chun Yee Chinese Society's Old People's Centre are now housed at 50 East India Dock Road, on the corner of Birchfield Street.

George Lansbury, Mayor of Poplar, cuts the first sod on the Chapel House Street estate housing scheme for building 120 houses on the Isle of Dogs, 13 January 1920. Lansbury was loved and admired in the East End, and despite losing his seat in Parliament in 1912 he continued to champion the cause of women and their right to vote. He then became editor of the *Daily Herald*, and after being re-elected as a Poplar councillor in November 1919 he led the councillors who refused to levy rates (in the Poplar Rates Dispute). As a result, the majority of the councillors were sent to prison for six weeks in September 1921.

A service being held in the ruins of the Poplar and Bromley Tabernacle, after its destruction by enemy action in March 1941. The 'Tab' was merged with Berger Hall, which was destroyed on the first day of the Blitz, and the church became known as the Poplar and Berger Baptist Tabernacle. Services were held in the Old Five Bells, a temperance pub owned by the Shaftesbury Society, until the new church in Teviot Street was opened in 1958.

Opposite: Mary Hughes (1860–1941) (seated, centre) with her friends. Mary was the daughter of Thomas Hughes, county court judge and author of *Tom Brown's Schooldays*. In 1895 she came to live with her sister in Whitechapel, where she devoted the rest of her life to helping the needy. A member of the Board of Guardians, a councillor and a JP, in 1918 her pacifism led her to become a Quaker. In the late 1920s Mary bought a pub, the Earl Grey in Vallance Road, and renamed it the Dewdrop Inn. It became a drop-in centre for local people. Mary Hughes died on 2 April 1941, just before a bombing raid destroyed much of the area she had lived in and loved so deeply.

Mary Ward, the second wife of John Ward, a soldier who fought in the Crimean War. Mary was in business as a staymaker in Cambridge Heath Road and was buried in Victoria Park Cemetery (now Meath Gardens).

Mary Ann Beckwith, daughter of Mary Ward. Mary Ann was a music teacher at the Birkbeck Schools in Cambridge Heath Road. Later she was a gentlefolks' companion before being married to a wine merchant in Westminster. She died of cancer and was buried in Kensal Green Cemetery.

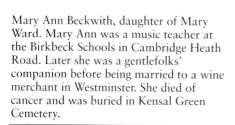

Miss Gormley, a Bethnal Green girl, beside the clock and ornaments presented to her by the police of Commercial Street Police Station (H) Whitechapel Division in recognition of her bravery in assisting a constable who was being violently assaulted by roughs, early 1900s. The umbrella in her left hand was presented to her on a previous occasion for a similar action.

Miss Rose Joseph, who won first prize at the first beauty show to be held in the East End, at Cambridge Music Hall, Spitalfields, August 1904. As the following portraits of the other prizewinners show, great attention was paid to their attire, as they were allowed no other means of improving their looks.

Miss Louise Hover, who won the second prize in the same beauty show. The rules of the contest stated that the girls were not permitted to wear any make-up whatsoever, but should display their natural beauty.

Miss Rose Cooper, the third prizewinner. There was also a consolation prize awarded. The contest proved so popular that the organizers decided to hold another one the following month.

Miss Rebecca Mayne, winner of the first prize at the second beauty show, open to all the East End and held at the Cambridge Music Hall, September 1904.

Father Joe Williamson with some of his parishioners in Cable Street, late 1950s. Father Williamson was a Poplar working-class boy who went on to become an Anglican priest. His parish in Cable Street was a notorious slum area, and his ministry there from 1952 to 1962 was dominated by the issues of slum housing and prostitution.

The Larkin family, about fifty in number, assembled for a wedding, 1920. They lived at No. 93 Bromley Street, which joins Stepney Way to Commercial Road. Mrs Larkin is prominent in the foreground, with her husband standing proudly beside her. The bride and groom are almost lost in the throng of relatives.

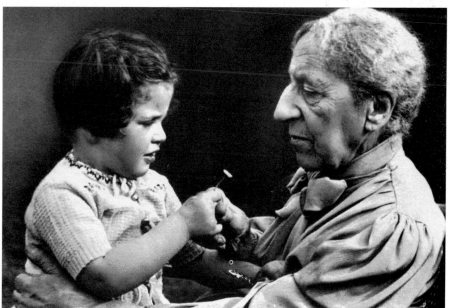

Alice Model (1856–1943) was a pioneer in the founding of nursing homes and health visiting. The maternity home she established in Underwood Street (later Underwood Road) became the Jewish Maternity Hospital. In 1896 she started a Jewish day nursery.

East Londoners at the ruined site of Single Street School in Stepney celebrate the second anniversary of the Battle of Britain. This picture was taken at the service held on 15 September 1942.

Acknowledgements

Many of the photographs we have selected are from the Whiffin Collection in Tower Hamlets Local History Library. We are grateful to the Local History Library for making available their extensive collection of photographs.

Acknowledgements are due also to the British Council, J. Connor (photographer), Fox Photos, the Greater London Record Office, the *Herald* newspaper, the Island History Trust Collection, Keystone, the Museum of London, the *New York Times*, Photo Source Ltd, Reuters, the Salvation Army International Heritage Centre, Stanley Shaw, John Topham Picture Library and the Whitechapel Mission.

Our thanks to Philip Mernick for contributions from his extensive postcard collection and to John Curtis for the pictures of the beauty queens.

We are especially grateful to Harry Watton at the Local History Library for his invaluable support and assistance.